THE LITTLE BOOK OF
LIFE'S
WISDOM

THE LITTLE BOOK OF

LIFE'S WISDOM

Personal inspiration from the author of *THE PROPHET*

KAHLIL GIBRAN

Published by Arrow Books in 2000

3 5 7 9 10 8 6 4

Copyright © Kahlil Gibran 1951, 1962, 1975.

Kahlil Gibran has asserted his right under the Copyright, Designs and Patents Act,
1988 to be identified as the author of this work

First published in the United Kingdom in 2000 by Arrow Books
Material in this book first appeared in the following books, also published by Arrow
Books:
A Treasury of Kahlil Gibran
A Second Treasury of Kahlil Gibran
A Third Treasury of Kahlil Gibran

Arrow Books
The Random House Group Limited
20 Vauxhall Bridge Road · London · SW1V 2SA

Random House Australia (Pty) Limited
20 Alfred Street · Milsons Point · Sydney · New South Wales 2061 · Australia

Random House New Zealand Limited
18 Poland Road · Glenfield · Auckland 10 · New Zealand

Random House (Pty) Limited
Endulini · 5a Jubilee Road · Parktown 2193 · South Africa

The Random House Group Limited Reg. No. 954009

www.randomhouse.co.uk

A CIP catalogue record for this book is available from the British Library

Papers used by Random House are natural, recyclable products made from wood
grown in sustainable forests. The manufacturing processes conform to the
environmental regulations of the country of origin

ISBN 0 09 941579 8

Designed by Lovelock & Co.
Printed and bound in Denmark by Nørhaven A/S, Viborg

Contents

Life and Love

Your daily life is your temple
and your religion,
Whenever you enter into it take
with you your all.

The Reality of Life is Life
itself, whose beginning is not
in the womb,
and whose ending is not in
the grave.

The first kiss is the first flower
at the tip of the branch of the
Tree of Life.

Love gives naught but itself
and takes naught but from itself.
Love possesses not nor would
it be possessed;
For love is sufficient unto love.

Beauty is life when life
unveils her holy face
But you are life and you are
the veil.

Love is the offspring of spiritual
affinity and unless that affinity is
created in a moment,
it will not be created in years
or even generations.

Love is a divine knowledge
that enables men to see as
much as the gods.

The song of the voice is sweet, but the song of the heart is the pure voice of heaven.

Love has no other desire but
to fulfil itself.

Let there be no purpose
in friendship
Save the deepening of the spirit.

Love is that holy wine which
the gods distill from their hearts
and pour into the hearts of men.

Those whom Love has not chosen as followers do not hear when Love calls.

Life is not only a merriment;
Life is desire and determination.

**In keeping yourself with labour
you are in truth loving life.**

Silence is one of the mysteries of love.

Love that opens our eyes and
enslaves our hearts can give us
the blessings of patience.

Man struggles to find life
outside himself,
unaware that the life he is
seeking is within him.

Limited love asks for
possession of the beloved,
but the unlimited asks only
for itself.

Love is the only flower
that grows and blossoms
without the aid of the seasons.

Old age is the snow of the
earth; it must,
through light and truth,
give warmth to the
seeds below, protecting them
and fulfilling their purpose.

On marriage:
Love one another, but make
not a bond of love:
Let it rather be a moving sea
between the shores of your soul.

On marriage:
Give your hearts; but not
into each other's keeping.
For only the hand of Life can
contain your hearts.
And stand together yet
not too near together:
For the pillars of the
temple stand apart,
And the oak tree and the
cypress grow not in each
other's shadow.

Circumstances drive us on
In narrow paths by kismet hewn.

Think not you can direct
the course of love,
For love, if it finds you worth,
directs your course.

The power to
Love is God's greatest
gift to man,
For it never will be
taken from the
Blessed one who loves.

When love beckons
to you, follow him,
Though his ways are hard
and steep.

I shall follow the path to
wherever my destiny
and my mission for Truth
shall take me.

Knowledge
and Wisdom

A wise man approaches
with his torch to
light up the path of mankind.

No man can reveal to you
aught but that which already
lies half asleep in the dawning
of your knowledge.

Learning is the only wealth
tyrants cannot despoil.

You may chain my hands
and shackle my feet;
you may even throw me into
a dark prison, but you
shall not enslave my thinking
because it is free.

Seek counsel of the aged,
for their eyes have
looked on the faces of the
years and their ears
have hearkened to the
voices of life.

He who does not seek
advice is a fool.
His folly blinds him to Truth
and makes him evil,
stubborn and a danger to
his fellow man.

Knowledge is your true patent
of nobility, no matter
who your father or what your
race may be.

You give but little when you
give of your possessions.
It is when you give of yourself
that you truly give.

Keep me away from the
wisdom which does not cry, the
philosophy which does not laugh
and the greatness which does not
bow before children.

Wisdom is not in words;
Wisdom is meaning within words.

Knowledge and understanding
are life's faithful companions
who will never prove untrue
to you.

Knowledge is your crown, and
understanding your staff;
and when they are with you, you
can possess no greater treasures.

Perplexity is the beginning
of knowledge.

Braving obstacles and
hardships is nobler than
retreat to tranquillity.

Know your own true worth,
and you shall not perish.

The true wealth of a nation
lies not in its gold or
silver but in its learning,
wisdom and in the
uprightness of its sons.

The supreme teaching
that changed the course
of humanity were the ideas
of a man whose genius
separated him from
his environment.

If your knowledge teaches
you not the value of things,
and frees you not from the
bondage to matter,
you shall never come near
the throne of truth.

Be wise - let Reason, not
Impulse be your guide.

Make haste slowly, and do not be slothful when opportunity beckons. Thus you will avoid grave errors.

A little knowledge that *acts* is worth infinitely more than much knowledge that is idle.

A man's merit lies in his
knowledge and in his deeds,
not in his colour, faith, race
or descent.

I abstain from the people who
consider insolence bravery and
tenderness cowardice.
And I abstain from those who
consider chatter wisdom and
silence ignorance.

I look up high to see
only the light,
And never look down to
see my shadow.
This is wisdom which
man must learn.

Will ever the day come when
the wise link the joy of
knowledge to youth's dream?

Appearance
and
Perception

Thoughts have a higher dwelling place than the visible world.

How small is the life of the
person, who places his hands
between his face and the world,
seeing naught but the narrow
lines of his hands.

In the house of Ignorance
there is no mirror in which
to view your soul.

Happiness is a myth we seek.

The appearance of
things changes according
to the emotions,
and thus we see magic
and beauty in them,
while the magic and beauty
are really within ourselves.

He who does not see the
angels and devils in the beauty
and malice of life will be far
removed from knowledge,
and his spirit will be empty
of affection.

Hell is not in torture;
Hell is in an empty heart.

Is not faith the sense of the
heart as truly as sight is the
sense of the eye?

Imagination finds a road
to the realm of the gods,
and there man can glimpse
that which is to be
after the soul's liberation from
the world of substance.

Not all of us are enabled to
see with our inner eyes
the great depths of life, and
it is cruel to demand that
the weak-sighted see the dim
and the far.

When the whirlwinds of youth
blow dust and sand,
the eyes are blind for a time.

The greater your joy
or your sorrow,
the smaller the world
in your eyes.

The idea is a segment
of knowledge that cannot be
proved with figures and words,
for it is too high and spacious
to be imprisoned at that
moment; too deeply imbedded
in the spiritual to submit yet
to the real.

Hearts know in silence
the secrets of the days
and the nights.

Every thing we see today,
made by past generations, was,
before its appearance, a
thought in the mind of a man
or an impulse in the heart
of a woman.

Everything that a man does secretly in the darkness of night will be clearly revealed in daylight.

If you close your eyes you
will perceive all things through
the depths of your inner self,
and you will see the world
physical and ethereal, in its
intended entirety.

Our appearance, our words,
our actions are never greater
than ourselves.
For the soul is our house;
our eyes its windows; and our
words its messengers.

Reason is light in darkness, as anger is darkness amidst light.

Time and place are spiritual
states, and all that is seen and
heard is spiritual.

How unjust to themselves
are those who turn their
backs to the sun,
and see naught except
the shadows of their physical
selves upon the earth!

Man and
God

Is it really God that created
Man, or is it the opposite?

God has made many doors
opening into truth which
He opens to all who knock upon
them with hands of faith.

The good in man should
freely flow.

Humanity is the spirit of the
Supreme Being on earth.

There is a desire deep within
the soul which drives man
from the seen to the unseen,
to philosophy and to the divine.

He who sees his real self
sees the truth of real life
for himself,
for all humanity, and
for all things.

We are the breath and
the fragrance of God.

A woman's happiness does
not come through man's
glory and honour,
nor through his generosity
and affection,
but through love that unites
both of their hearts and
affections,
making them one member of
life's body and one word upon
the lips of God.

You and I are all children
of one faith,
for the divers paths of religion
are fingers of the
loving hand of one Supreme
Being, a hand
extended to all, offering
completeness of spirit to all,
eager to receive all.

The wise man is he who
loves and reveres God.

Your house is your larger body.
It grows in the sun and sleeps
in the stillness of the night
and it is not dreamless.

You are the bows from
which your children as
living arrows are sent forth.

The things which the child
loves remain in the domain
of the heart until old age.

The most beautiful thing in
life is that our souls remain
hovering over the places where
we once enjoyed ourselves.

Man is weak by his own hand,
for he
has refashioned God's law into
his own confining manner of life.

He who does not see the kingdom
of heaven in this life will never
see it in the coming life.

Between the spiritual world
and the world of substance
there is a path upon which we
walk in a swoon of slumber.

Man possesses a destiny
Which impels his thoughts and
Actions and words, and that not
Sufficing, directs his footsteps to
A place of unwilling abode.

God has given you knowledge,
so that by its light
you may not only worship
him but also see yourself
in your weakness and strength.

Man is empowered by God
to hope and hope fervently,
until that for which he is
hoping takes the cloak of
oblivion from his eyes,
whereupon he will at last
view his real self.

The believer lives for all the days and the nights and the unfaithful live but a few hours.

Make Beauty your religion, and
worship her as your godhead;
for she is the visible, manifest
and perfect handiwork of God.

Will man remain a slave of
self-confinement
until the end of the world?
Or will he be freed by
the passing of time
and live in the Spirit for
the Spirit?

If you would know God, be
not therefore a solver of riddles.
Rather look about you and
you shall see Him playing with
your children.

God is the expression of the
intelligent universe.

Nature and
the Universe

Everything in creation
exists within you,
And everything in you
exists within creation.

Nature reaches out to us
with welcoming arms and
bids us enjoy her beauty.

Why must Man destroy
what Nature has built?

If we suffer, our pain lies
not in our wounds,
but in the very heart of nature.

The mountains, trees and
rivers change their appearance
with the vicissitudes of times
and seasons,
as a man changes with his
experiences and emotions.

In every winter's heart there
is a quivering spring, and
behind the veil of each night
there is a smiling dawn.

Everything on earth lives
according to the law of nature,
and from that law emerges the
glory and joy of liberty.

Look at the Darkness,
giving birth to the sun.

Speak not of peoples
and laws and Kingdoms,
for the whole earth
is my birthplace
and all humans are my brothers.

The earth that opens wide
her mouth to swallow
man and his works is
the redeemer of our
souls from bondage to
our bodies.

Everything in nature
bespeaks the mother.

The mother, the prototype
of all existence,
is the eternal spirit, full
of beauty and love.

The sun is the mother
of earth and gives it its
nourishment of heat;
it never leaves the universe
at night until it has put
the earth to sleep
to the song of the sea and the
hymn of birds and brooks.

The flowers of the field are
the children of sun's affection
and nature's love;
and the children of men are the
flowers of love and compassion.

Spring is the spirit of an
unknown God speeding
through the world.

The river continues
on its way to the sea,
broken by the wheel of
the mill or not.

This earth is the mother
of trees and flowers.
It produces them, nurses
them and weans them.
The trees and flowers
become mothers of their
great fruits and seeds.

Beauty brings your heart closer
to the throne of woman,
who is the mirror of your
affections and the teacher of
heart in the ways of Nature,
which is your life's home.

Like a giant oak tree
covered with apple blossoms
is the vast man in you.
His might binds you to the
earth, his fragrance lifts
you into space,
and in his durability you
are deathless.

Art and Beauty

Art is one step from the visibly known toward the unknown.

Beauty is not in the face
Beauty is a light in the heart.

Imagination is the only creator,
its nearest and dearest
manifestation is Art.

Art is life, life is art;
all else is trite and empty
in comparison.

Beauty is that which
attracts your soul,
and that which loves to give
and not to receive.

Where shall you seek beauty,
and how shall
you find her unless she herself
be your way and your guide?

Every beauty and greatness
in this world
is created by a single thought
or emotion inside a man.

Beauty is eternity gazing
at itself in a mirror.
But you are eternity and
you are the mirror.

Art is forced to create for
expressing itself.

Poet, examine your crown
of thorns; you will
Find concealed in it a
budding wreath of laurel.

When you meet Beauty, you
feel that the hands deep within
your inner self are stretched
forth to bring her into the
domain of your heart.

Only our spirits can understand
beauty, or live and grow with it.

Beauty has its own
heavenly language,
loftier than the voices
of tongues and lips.

Real beauty lies in the
spiritual accord that is called
love which can exist between
a man and a woman.

The subtlest beauties in our
life are unseen and unheard.

Art, through drawing a
line between the beautiful
and the ugly,
is the nearest way to God.

Beauty is that harmony
between joy and sorrow
which begins in our holy of
holies and ends beyond
the scope of our imagination.

Through my soul let music ring;
For song is the arm of love
Descending in beauty from
God above.

One hour devoted to the
pursuit of Beauty
And Love is worth a full
century of glory
Given by the frightened
weak to the strong.

Life is naked. A nude body is the truest and noblest symbol of life.

Real beauty is a ray which
emanates from the holy of
holies of the spirit, and
illuminates the body,
as life comes from the depths
of the earth and gives colour
and scent to a flower.

Death and Freedom

Death is an ending to the son of
the earth, but to the soul it is
the start, the triumph of life.

You can only be free when even
the desire of seeking freedom
becomes a harness to you,
and when you cease to
speak of freedom as a goal
and a fulfilment.

Life without Freedom is like
a body without a soul.

Life, Freedom and Thought are three-in-one, and are everlasting and never pass away.

God has given you a spirit
with wings on which to soar
into the spacious firmament
of Love and Freedom.

He who lives a single Springtime
Is like one who lives for ages.

Only those return to Eternity
Who on earth seek out Eternity.

If I did not covet immortality,
I would never have learned
the song
which has been sung through
all of time.

The oppressed prisoner, who
can break away from his jail
and does not do so, is a coward.

Dying for Freedom is
nobler than living
in the shadow of weak
submission.

He who does not prefer exile to slavery is not free by any measure of freedom, truth and duty.

He who embraces death
with the sword
Of truth in his hand will
eternalise
With the Eternity of Truth.
For Life
Is weaker than Death
and Death is
Weaker than Truth.

Between the people of
eternity and people of the earth
there is a constant
communication, and all
comply with the will of that
unseen power.

Each thing that exists
remains forever, and the
very existence of existence
is proof of its eternity.

The yearning of my heart tells
me there is peace in the grave.

A child in the womb, no
sooner born than returned
to earth - such is the fate
of man, the fate of nations
and of the sun, the moon,
and the stars.

Man is like the foam of
the sea, that floats upon the
surface of the water. When
the wind blows, it
vanishes, as if it had never
been. Thus are our
lives blown away by death.

Life and death are one, even as
the river and the sea are one.

You shall be free indeed
when your days are
not without a care nor
your nights without a want
and a grief,
But rather when these
things girdle your life and
yet you rise above them
naked and unbound.

Life is weaker than Death,
and Death is Weaker than Love.

Whenever you pass by the
field where you have laid your
ancestors look well thereupon,
and you shall see yourselves
and your children dancing
hand in hand.

Go back to the joy of your
dwellings
and you will find there
that which Death cannot
remove from you and me.

For what is to die but to stand
naked in the wind and to melt
into the sun?